STEM Superst

# George Washington Carver

by Michelle Parkin

NORWOOD HOUSE 🏠 PRESS

Cover: George Washington Carver made American farming better.

Norwood House Press
For information regarding Norwood House Press, please visit our website at:
www.norwoodhousepress.com or call 866-565-2900.

Hardcover ISBN: 978-1-68450-744-3
Paperback ISBN: 978-1-68404-822-9

**Library of Congress Cataloging-in-Publication Data**

Names: Parkin, Michelle, 1984- author.
Title: George Washington Carver / by Michelle Parkin.
Description: [Chicago] : Norwood House Press, [2023] | Series: Stem
    superstars | Includes index. | Audience: Ages 5-8 | Audience: Grades K-1
    | Summary: "Describes the life and work of George Washington Carver, a
    plant scientist who advanced American farming practices"-- Provided by
    publisher.
Identifiers: LCCN 2022041773 (print) | LCCN 2022041774 (ebook) | ISBN
    9781684507443 (hardcover) | ISBN 9781684048229 (paperback) | ISBN
    9781684048427 (epub)
Subjects: LCSH: Carver, George Washington, 1864?-1943--Juvenile literature.
    | African American agriculturists--Biography--Juvenile literature. |
    Agriculturists--United States--Biography--Juvenile literature. |
    Inventors, Black--United States--Biography--Juvenile literature. |
    Inventors--United States--Biography--Juvenile literature.
Classification: LCC S417.C3 P357 2023  (print) | LCC S417.C3  (ebook) | DDC
    630.92 [B]--dc23/eng/20220831
LC record available at https://lccn.loc.gov/2022041773
LC ebook record available at https://lccn.loc.gov/2022041774

359N–012023
Manufactured in the United States of America in North Mankato, Minnesota.

# ★ Table of Contents ★

# Chapter 1

# Early Life

George Carver was born in the 1860s. No one knows the date. Not even Carver! Carver's family lived in Missouri. They were **enslaved** people.

There is a statue of Carver close to where he was born.

GEORGE WASHINGTON CARVER

Carver grew up in this farmhouse in Missouri.

**Did You Know?**
Slavery ended in America on December 18, 1865.

When Carver was a baby, he was kidnapped. His mother and sister were taken too. People wanted to sell them. Carver was rescued. But he never saw his mother or sister again.

Carver loved plants. He wanted to learn about them. He wanted to go to school. Black and white students were **separated**. Carver went to an all-Black school.

**Carver's all-Black schoolhouse was small, with only two rooms.**

# Chapter 2

# Plant Professor

Carver finished high school in 1880. He tried to go to Highland College in Kansas. But the school found out Carver was Black. They said he couldn't come.

Carver was also a painter. He liked to paint plants.

11

Carver faced **racism**. But he didn't give up. He was accepted at a different college. Carver was the first Black student. He studied **botany**. Later, he was the first Black professor there.

Carver's new college focused on farm science. It is now called Iowa State University.

**Tuskegee Institute is in Alabama. It is the second-oldest Black college there.**

Did You Know?
The "W" in Carver's name now stands for "Washington."

Booker T. Washington was a teacher. He fought racism too. He helped start the Tuskegee Institute. It was an all-Black college. Carver taught there for 47 years.

# Chapter 3

# Famous Scientist

In the South, many farmers only grew cotton. Carver saw that doing this hurt the **soil**. He told farmers what to do. They could plant other **crops** every other year. Peanuts and sweet potatoes made the soil healthy again.

**Carver traveled to farms and taught farmers how to help their crops, like cotton, grow better.**

**Carver found 118 ways to use sweet potatoes. One way was using sweet potatoes to make glue for stamps!**

Farmers were worried they wouldn't make as much money. Carver had a plan. He found more than 300 uses for peanuts. They could be used for food. They could also make shampoo and shaving cream! Farmers could earn money with these ideas. Carver became famous.

**Did You Know?**
Carver was the first Black person with a national **monument**.

Carver died on January 5, 1943. He spent his life helping people. His ideas have helped how we grow crops today.

Carver has inspired many people to study plant science.

21

# ★ Career Connections ★

1 Historians study the lives of people from the past. Imagine you are a historian. Research someone you like who lived long ago.

2 Carver studied botany in school. Botanists study plants. Look at a plant or flower near your home. With an adult, go to your local library. Ask a librarian to help you learn more about it.

3 Carver found more than 300 ways to use peanuts. Food science is the study of food. Food scientists use different ways to learn about the food we eat. Imagine you are a food scientist. With an adult's help, look online for some fun food experiments to try at home.

4 Carver helped farmers make their crops grow. Agronomists study soil and crops. With an adult's help, go online and learn more about this career.

# ★ Glossary ★

**botany** (BOT-uh-nee): The scientific study of plants.

**crops** (KROPZ): Plants grown in large amounts, usually for food.

**enslaved** (en-SLAYVD): Owned as a slave.

**monument** (MON-yuh-muhnt): A statue that is meant to remind people of an event or person.

**racism** (RAY-siz-uhm): When people are treated unfairly because of their skin color or background.

**separated** (SEP-uh-rate-ed): Split apart.

**slavery** (SLAYV-ur-ee): The practice of people being owned by others and thought of as property.

**soil** (SOYL): Dirt that plants can grow in.

# ★ For More Information ★

### Books

Amin, Anita Nahta. *Elon Musk*. STEM Superstars. Chicago, IL: Norwood House Press, 2021. Read this book to learn about the life of the famous inventor, Elon Musk.

Jazynka, Kitson. *George Washington Carver*. Washington, D.C.: National Geographic, 2016. Learn about George Washington Carver's life.

### Websites

**George Washington Carver**
(https://kids.nationalgeographic.com/history/article/george-washington-carver)
Read interesting facts about George Washington Carver and his life.

**George Washington Carver National Monument**
(www.nps.gov/gwca/planyourvisit/justforkids.htm) Find out about the George Washington Carver National Monument.

# ★ Index ★

# ★ About the Author ★

Michelle Parkin is an editor and a children's book author. She has written more than 15 children's books about famous people, animals, and dinosaurs. She lives with her daughter and golden retriever mix in Minnesota.